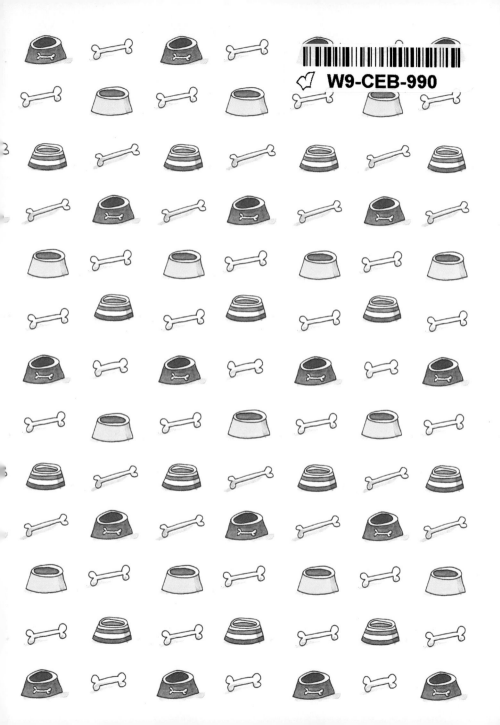

breeds

a canine Compendium

Fenella Smith
and
The Brothers McLeod

FLATIRON
BOOKS
NEW YORK

www.flatironbooks.com

The Library of Congress Cataloging-in-Publication Data is available upon request.

ISBN 978-1-250-06633-6 (paper over board)
ISBN 978-1-250-06634-3 (e-book)

Originally published in the United Kingdom by Square Peg.

Flatiron books may be purchased for educational, business, or promotional use.

For information on bulk purchases, please contact Macmillan Corporate and Premium Sales Department at 1-800-221-7945, extension 5442, or write
Specialmarkets@macmillan.com

First U.S. Edition: October 2015

10 9 8 7 6 5 4 3 2 1

We three siblings grew up in a household that at one time or another had two guinea pigs, a rabbit, two chickens, about fifteen stick insects, three goldfish, a whole shoal of tropical fish, four cats, and three dogs. This is surely a testimony to our mother's love of animals and, considering our father's allergy to most animals, a testimony to our father's love of our mother.

Our first dog arrived in 1985 when I was only ten. She was a West Highland White Terrier called Suzie. Shortly after she was joined by Sophie, a bat-eared Yorkshire Terrier. The cat wasn't impressed. I wasn't either. When Suzie arrived I remember being quite baffled. I had really wanted a dog, but my idea of a dog was fairly fixed. Dogs were big and yellow (basically were Golden Retrievers) or were very yappy and shaped like a black sausage (like our Auntie Pam's dachshund 'Zonty'). They were not small, white and cute. Despite this early setback I grew to love Suzie very much (aside from her ear-splitting bark and her love of rolling in noxious substances). She was a wonderful dog, spirited, full of energy and very loving. And since then, our family has included a Cairn, a Border Terrier, a Border Collie and a Black Labrador.

My brothers and I had rather an idyllic childhood; wonderfully fun parents, many pets and a freedom of childhood that seems to be less available to children of today with the interference of technology.

It is through our parents' encouragement to be true to our individual selves and interests that we have all turned out with very different skills and perspectives on the world, yet we are the best of friends. Writing this book with my brothers has been a process of learning (Myles, who is very clever, taught me all about the DNA plasticity of dogs), laughter (Greg and his wonderfully bonkers view on the world through his amazing drawing) and respect (for my two elder incredibly talented brothers). We have loved writing it, I hope you enjoy reading it. It's a combination of rather interesting and useful facts, with a little bit of silliness. Much like our family really.

— Fenella Smith

Of course I now know that dogs come in all shapes and sizes. Thanks to the plasticity of the dog genome, these domesticated wolves can be as small as a Chihuahua or as tall as a Great Dane. Dogs are truly the most extraordinary animals. Imagine if humans were as varied in size, colour, shape and strength! Researching for this book revealed to us that dogs were even more diverse than we knew. Before we began, I'd never heard of the fork-nosed Catalburun, the hairless Peruvian Inca Orchid or the climbing Telomian.

Strictly speaking, to be a breed of dog you need to belong to the species Canis lupus familiaris. This book does include a few wild dogs from other species — things like dire wolves, foxes and jackals (dog cousins if you like!) just because we thought they were rather interesting too.

My sister Fenella and I had great fun writing the entries, and it has been a joy to see what our older brother Greg came up with when he started illustrating them. The book is a celebration of the dog, in its many forms. We hope you recognise some of the canine characters here from your own life, as well as discovering some new exotic friends.

— Myles McLeod

Affenpinscher

Known as the monkey-dog or
little devil with a moustache.
One of those lovely little dogs
that thinks it's a bigger dog.
Come and have a go if you think
you're tough enough!

Afghan Hound

Tall, elegant and well behaved
dogs with excellent eyesight.
Have a tendency to be slightly
aloof. Will require shampoo
and set (curlers optional).

African Wild Dog (wild dog)

Nuttier than a squirrel's burp.
Wild in the 'would-probably-
actually-eat-you' kind of way.
Sadly, endangered these days.

Airedale Terrier

Known as the King of Terriers, this breed is intelligent and loves to hunt. Distinguished by their lengthy, flat snout and masterly posture. Have the air of a very confident teddy bear.

Akita

Loyal and playful dogs with
the softest ears known to
man. Once used for babysitting
children while parents worked in
the rice paddies. Basically a
cuddly ninja.

Alaskan klee kai

Looks like a Siberian Husky
that shrunk in the wash.
Clever, sprightly breed that
needs close training to
prevent small-dog syndrome.
Don't expect them to pull a
sled: Far too pretty for that.

Alaskan Malamute

The largest Arctic dog and descended from the Arctic wolf. The soldiers of the dog world, will pull heavy, loaded sleds through the most severe wintry conditions. If fenced in they'll just dig their way out in search of the Far North.

American Bulldog

Quite a dog! They can jump a vertical height of seven feet, are very emotional and bond deeply with their owner. Can be aloof with strangers but make excellent working and/or guard dogs. They can also whistle the National Anthem. Proudly.

American Eskimo Dog

Silly name, really, as it's neither American nor an Eskimo. Originates from Northern Europe. These dogs are pure white, very clever and have a tendency to bark at strangers. Come in toy and miniature versions for handbags and laps.

Anatolian Shepherd

A Turkish breed which, remarkably,
is able to guard and move herds of
livestock without human direction.
Available for Nativity bookings.

Arctic Fox (wild dog)

Look so incredibly cute but wouldn't make a great house pet as they'd try and sleep in the freezer and potentially eat your other pets. They are especially partial to ringed seal pup.

Australian Cattle Dog

Often known as Heelers, these
dogs round up cattle and get the
stragglers going by nipping at
their heels. Also known to nip
slow-moving humans. This breed
needs an active life so an agility
course around the house and
garden ought to do the trick.

Australian Shepherd

This happy, energetic breed needs
a good daily workout to keep it
smiling. It's had heaps of other names,
such as Bob-Tail, Pastor Dog, Spanish
Shepherd before settling on Australian
Shepherd. In fact, the Aussie is
actually American. Go figure!

Basset Hound

Sad-looking, inquisitive dogs with
an outgoing nature. Have the
potential to be unruly and bossy.
Look rather comical when running
and generally get picked last in
gym class. AW!

<u>Beagle</u>

Very jolly dogs. Beagles can just run and run, and quite frankly need to as they can put on the pounds if not exercised. You can often hear a pack of them on a Sunday in the countryside, not fox hunting of course.

Bearded Collie

This beardy is no weirdy.
Long-haired, exuberant, outgoing
and affectionate... like a
live-in hippy.

Beauceron

Supremely hardy dogs, athletic and able to sleep outside due to their waterproof double coat. They are excellent herding dogs but were also used in France, where they originated, for defending flocks from predators. They have double dewclaws, maybe for fighting wolves? Who knows!

Bedlington Terrier

This graceful, cuddly breed is a
master of disguise! Why? Because,
with its white, woolly coat the
Bedlington is the archetypal wolf
in sheep's clothing. Mind you, in
temperament it's less like a lamb
and more like a mule.

Belgian Malinois

A high-achiever in the dog world.
Hugely active and intelligent dogs that
make the fast-track recruitment
into working for the police and
military. Love to remain close to
their owners, but will tell on you
if you're up to no good.

Bernese Mountain Dog

Totally unaware of its humungous size and never seems to grow out of the puppy phase; though this is just a cover for a secret identity. All Bernese are actually superheroes and members of a secret rescue organisation based in Switzerland.

Bichon Frisé

Not the sharpest tool in the box but they do make up for it in looks. That puffball effect requires a lot of effort. Their curly hypoallergenic hair requires backcombing to make it stand on end (and maybe a little hairspray when no one's looking).

Black Labrador

Deeply affectionate, mildly daft with a tendency to eat everything in sight. You can have hours of fun watching them belly-flop into water chasing after tennis balls. As they age they may become a bit grey and fat. A running machine and Just For Men can resolve these issues.

Black Mouth Cur

American, very loyal and really
rather versatile. They love to
hunt and will happily spend hours
looking up a tree trying to outstare
a squirrel. Disney's Old Yeller was
a Black Mouth Cur. That's your
useful fact of the day.

Bloodhounds

You know the Bloodhound; it's the one with the really droopy face. Like dogged detectives (pun intended) will ceaselessly follow the scent especially of deer or wild boar. They have also been used to track humans, which is why the Scots used to call this breed the Sleuth-Hound.

Border Collie

The cleverest dog there is.
They say they carry their brains
in their tails as their tails hang
low when they are working. Very
neurotic with a tendency towards
OCD. Excellent at rounding up
children on the playground.

Border Terrier

A small breed with long, strong, restless legs, the Border will not hesitate to remind you it's walkies time; though on hot days, will settle for upside-down sunbathing. This dog shuns woofs and barks in favour of snorts and whines. Also, does a good impression of a meerkat.

Borzoi

The wolf-hunter of Russia,
this wonderfully tall and swift
breed was once used in hunts
with packs of over a hundred
dogs! These days they prefer to
relax by the fire and read Tolstoy.

Boston Terrier

Compact and sprightly dog.
With their short snouts they
tend to snore and can even do
a reverse sneeze (great party
trick). Disproportionately massive
ears. Be warned: they can hear
you talking about them, even
when you're whispering.

Bouvier des Flandres

Deluxe name, deluxe dog.
A large, good-natured farm
or city dog from Belgium that
comes in a variety of colours.
If you need to work out where
the head is among that rich
double coat, just look for the
pink tongue.

Boxer

The Boxer is a boisterous
clown, though he's happy too.
Rumour has it that in London
some stand on two feet, wear
uniforms and disguise themselves
as police constables.

Briard

Really clever and very loving.
They hail from the French region
of Brie. Used to carry supplies to
soldiers on the front line in the
First World War (presumably cheese).
How they did it is a mystery as
surely they can't see where
they're going with all that hair.

Brittany

Looks like a Spaniel on stilts.
A sensitive and often shy breed.
A useful retrieving dog if you
like shooting birdies.

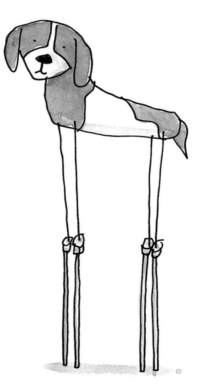

Brown Labrador

Have a reputation as being a little fatter and more stupid than their black counterparts. It's merely a ruse so they can spend more time curled up next to the fire. Make excellent footrests and are very good at cleaning kitchen floors. Will happily lick your plate clean, too.

Brussels Griffon

If you're feeling posh it's Griffon Bruxellois. This breed used to be kept by Belgian cab drivers to control vermin in stables. Not a terribly handsome hound if we're honest. Has a bit of a squished face and impressive overbite, but they are hugely affectionate and loyal.

Bull Terrier

White with the occasional patch,
Bull Terriers may look like the pirates
of the dog world, but they are in
fact fun-loving and good natured. They
don't like to be left alone, but, then,
who does?

Bulldog

Once a fighting dog used for
bull - baiting. Yikes! Like a
friendly old wrestler who's mellowed
with time.

Cairn Terrier

Cute and sprightly, available in orange and brown. Can be a bit dense and confused at times. Careful not to mistake the orange ones for a duster.

Canaan Dog

Israel's national dog, they are
thought to have existed for
millennia and are seen on
ancient texts and drawings.
Interestingly, this breed can still
be found in the wild! They love
a party and can often be heard
howling in the distance.

Cane Corso

A real soldier, this robust chap
is descended from Roman war dogs!
Favourite fancy dress costume:
gladiator.

Cat

This book disgusts me.

Catahoula Leopard Dog

Legend has it the multi coloured Catahoula is a sixteenth-century cross-breed of European and Native American dogs. They used to be the Catahoula Cur, but after being appointed as the state dog for Louisiana, the Governor promoted them to Leopard.

Çatalburun

With their peculiar split noses,
these Turkish Pointers are unlikely
to win a beauty contest. In fact,
their name means literally
'Fork Nose'. Rather like
Quasimodo, they might not be
pretty, but they still need a lot
of love!

Cavalier King Charles Spaniel

A very pretty breed of spaniel that absolutely loves human interaction. Hasn't a single aggressive bone in its body, although, being Cavaliers, they are pretty handy with a sword.

Chesapeake Bay Retriever

The water-loving Chessies are descended from two canine survivors of an English shipwreck off the coast of Maryland. Want a lazy lapdog?

Then look elsewhere.

Chihuahua

Teeny—weeny dogs originating in Mexico with a quite remarkable history dating back thousands of years. Preferred by a certain type of society gal. This cute breed has a bit of a temper and can often be seen having a tantrum inside a designer tote.

Chinese Crested Dog

Some dogs have selective hearing; this one has selective hair. Entirely hairless apart from their heads, tail and paws. Will happily wear a Barbour jacket in winter.

Chow Chow

Legend says this Chinese dog
has a bluish tongue because it
licked up pieces of sky at the
dawn of time. They're
certainly an old breed. In fact,
Chow Chows were once eaten
as a delicacy. Not to be
confused with Chow Mein.

Cockapoo

A charming mix of a Cocker
Spaniel and Poodle. Known in
the US since the 1950's, this
cute, cuddly cross-breed comes in
a variety of shapes and colours.
Will wake you up at dawn with
a cry of 'Cock-a-poodle-do'.

Cocker Spaniel

The most popular Spaniel breed.
Their name comes from their
original job: flushing and
retrieving woodcock. These days
these happy, lively dogs are more
likely to retrieve your slippers.

Coton de Tulear

The Royal Dog of Madagascar
no less! Basically looks like an
explosion in a cotton factory.

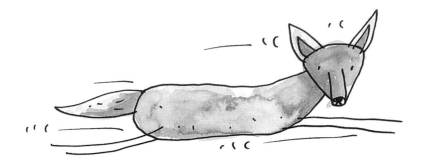

Coyote (wild dog)

These North Americans are savvy and swift. They can run at forty miles per hour, which seems excessive when you like to hunt frogs, insects and fruit. Actually, they eat pretty much anything. Must be why they're so successful (unless they're chasing roadrunners).

Czechoslovakian Vlcak

First bred in an experiment in
1955 in the Czechoslovak Socialist
Republic. Alsatians were crossed
with Carpathian wolves! They
have great endurance and have been
tracked running for sixty miles in
just eight hours. Unfit mailmen
beware!

Dachshund

A long, loving and inquisitive dog. Slightly neurotic, will spend large parts of the day worrying. Make excellent draft stoppers.

Dalmatian

The famously spotty one,
though pups are born white. Started
out life as a 'carriage dog' running
alongside Regency coaches. A
Dalmatian's steady gaze suggests
it knows a great deal more than you,
and possibly has a Ph.D.

Dingo (wild dog)

Dingoes are a subspecies of
Grey Wolf. They aren't really kept
as pets and are a bit on the wild
side, but, then, so would you be
if you ate wallabies and had to
keep an eye open for crocodiles.

Dire Wolf (wild dog)

The bad news: this is the
heaviest canine ever, up to
five feet long with massive
teeth and a small brain.
The good news: they died out
10,000 years ago. Phew!

Doberman

This Pinscher breed was developed
by a German tax collector who
wanted to discourage late
payers. They are smart, strong
and skillful trackers. So pay
up promptly!

Dogue de Bordeaux

Has the largest head of all the canines, with loose wrinkly skin. Makes them look endearingly confused.

English Mastiff

Not so much mastiff as
MASSIVE! Born to guard,
they need strong human leadership
and to be well socialised. Not
a good bedroom companion as
they tend to snore loudly.

Finnish Lapphund

This obedient breed comes from Lapland and is traditionally used to herd reindeer. Santa's favourite dog.

Finnish Spitz

A foxy coloured guard dog, this breed competes in barking competitions in their native Finland. If you think Spitz is an unfortunate name, try saying their old one, Suomenpystykorva.

Flat-coated Retriever

Closely related to the Labrador,
but with a flat, silky, shiny
coat that makes all the other
breeds jealous. Great family
dogs that love to work, too.
Used to be a favourite of
fishermen, which explains their
love for swimming.

Fox (wild dog)

There are almost thirty
species loosely identified as
foxes. But all of them are
adaptable, alert and smart. So
smart they write themselves
into fairy stories as the cunning
characters. Also pretty smelly
thanks to their odoriferous
scent glands. Peeeew!

Fox Terrier

Come in smooth or wire-coated
flavours. Practically inexhaustible,
they are the Marco Polos of the
dog world because they just love
to explore. Of course, they
also love hunting rabbits, rats and
yes, foxes.

Foxhound

Most definitely a sociable
pack dog with huge stamina.
Often used for hunting. If they
were human you'd find them
propping up the bar, last man
standing, on a Friday night.

French Bulldog

Like a bulldog, but more chic.

German Shepherd

The commandos of the dog world. Once known as the Alsatian. Possibly the most popular breed of them all. Great friends, formidable enemies. Which explains why almost 50,000 of them were signed up to the German army in the First World War!

Goldador

Sounds like a James Bond villain but is in fact a mixture of a Golden Labrador and a Golden Retriever so they are super-adorable and super-clever. They also make excellent guide and assistance dogs. Straight As at school for this breed.

Golden Retriever

The supermodel of the dog world,
they get all the best TV jobs.
Other dogs lure them into muddy
puddles to even things out a little.

Gordon Setter

This breed is very handsome
indeed with a fine black and
tan, silky, fluffy coat and strong
muzzle. Gordon Setters are
related to Irish and English
Setters; no one's sure who
Gordon is, though.

Great Dane

This gentle giant is a great
friend, though sadly short-lived.
On a cold evening, it may shield
the warmth of the fire from
everyone else. Also, it's
probably worth buying your Dane
its own settee if you ever
want to sit down again.

Great Pyrenees

Is it a dog or a polar bear?
If you'd like a pet polar bear, get
one of these. Huge, white and
fluffy. Plus they won't eat you.
They just love to be loved.

Grey Wolf

The mother of all our domesticated breeds and still the largest, it's the Grey Wolf. They don't actually howl at the moon, though they do like to sing together at night. Their calls can carry up to ten miles — useful if you lose the rest of the pack. kind of like a doggy GPS.

Greyhound

With a top speed of forty miles
per hour, the sweet-natured
Greyhound is the fastest breed
around. Ancient Egyptian tomb
carvings reveal they may be one of
the longest lived, too. Talking of
carvings, in the USA all racing
Greyhounds get a tattoo.
    Rock on!

Havanese

This toy breed is Cuba's national dog and just loves to be the centre of attention. The breed has a voluminous silky coat that comes in all colours. The white variety is sometimes mistaken for a ghost.

Ibizan Hound

Like a Fox Terrier it can have
a smooth or wiry coat. Graceful
as a deer, with striking amber
eyes and ears big enough to pick
up radio signals. Favourite music:
Trance, Techno, Spanish Guitar.

Irish Red and White Setter

Without a generous amount of exercise this athletic, independent gundog will make its own entertainment, probably by destroying your stuff. They have zero guarding instinct, but that makes them great friends and good with kids.

Irish Terrier

A reckless daredevil with a big heart. Has a warm, wiry double coat to protect it from the dependable Irish weather.

Tells good jokes.

Irish Wolfhound

A very old breed, often used as
a war hound. As the tallest breed
in the world they need a generous
amount of space for exercise.
They are hugely affectionate, often
even to strangers. Will frequently
take delight at running full pelt
into someone new to say hello.

Jack Russell Terrier

Small, muscular and happy to
shout at any dog or human
that passes by. Has a reputation
in the dog world as a bit of a
bully, but is really quite
timorous. They hate being left
alone and secretly just want
to be everyone's best bud.

Jackal (wild dog)

The beautiful, slender Jackals
like to sleep in the day and go
out for an evening breakfast of
insects, small mammals and
already dead, decaying stuff. Nice.

Jug

No, not a kind of pottery, but
a cross between a Jack Russell
and a Pug. This happy hybrid is
curious and active, but also loves
a cuddle.

Karelian Bear Dog

This Finnish breed is hardcore.
It may look like a cuddly collie, but
it can hunt bears. Yes, bears.
Keen, intelligent eyes, black and
white straight fur and fluffy,
curly-whirly tail that folds
over itself.

King Charles Spaniel

Smaller than the Cavalier
breed and snub-nosed. But is
there anything silkier? They
haven't really moved on since
the Restoration, and are partial
to croquet, afternoon tea and
Baroque music.

Komondor

A Hungarian guard dog used to
life on the wide open plains.
Despite their rather comical
appearance, these giant mops are
not to be trifled with. Definitely
not suited to town life — unless
you live in a street plagued by
wolves and bears.

Kuri

The now extinct kuri lived
in New Zealand until the
1800s. Their flesh was
considered a delicacy, and
according to the explorer
James Cook, they tasted
as good as lamb. Ugh!

Labradoodle

Possibly springier than a Springer Spaniel. So affectionate it may have two hearts (one Poodle, one Labrador). When sleeping on the sofa, may be mistaken for a fluffy pillow.

Lagotto Romagnolo

A gundog with a name fit for a Roman senator. They really appreciate the finer things in life which is why they love using their nose to hunt for truffles. Probably enjoys a good chianti, too. Buon appetito!

Lakeland Terrier

A hardy, sturdy breed born of
the Lake District. They can be
a little stubborn and will instantly
become deaf to you if there's
something more interesting to do.

Leonberger

The mayor of Leonberg bred
this dog to look like a lion in
honour of his town. Luckily,
that's where the big cat
connection ends; this gentle
giant will protect your
livestock, rather than have
it for dinner.

Lhasa Apso

While these dogs look like high maintenance fur balls with no brain, they were in fact bred as alert dogs to warn Buddhist monks of intruders. They aren't sleeping, they are meditating. Om.

Maltese

A toy breed. They look like a
toy and, if we're honest, seem
to have the brain of a toy.
However, this is an ancient breed,
so maybe they are just wiser than
all of us and are keeping quiet so
they don't have to round up sheep
or hunt things.

Maltipoo

Not a great name but, they are
pretty. Cross between a Toy
Poodle and Maltese. They are
so cutesy they don't look real,
but they are, they establish
this by yapping. A lot. Shush!

Maremma Sheepdog

Originates from Italy, big fella.

Not a breed for novices, they are tough, brave guard dogs tolerant of snow and known for being wolf-slayers. Not that they look fierce; they have a noble, aloof, yet reassuring face, rather like canine newsreaders.

New Guinea Singing Dog

Bit of a wild one this, though very handsome. Likes to sing instead of bark and can control the pitch of its howl. Sounds something like a ghost's wail or a flapping door with a rusty hinge. So, rather like opera.

Newfoundland

Massive and wonderfully stoic
dogs. Originally bred to assist
fishermen in Newfoundland, Canada.
Have a remarkably good waterproof
coat and huge webbed feet. They
drool like no other dog on earth
(Newfoundland drool bibs are
available to purchase). Take
cover when they shake.

Norfolk Terrier

Compact little ratters that
aren't afraid of larger adversaries
Having said that, this hardy breed
is friendly and less likely to
start a fight than many other
terriers. How civilised!

Norwegian Lundehund

Smart, snuggly and happy to pee anywhere. Their amazing bendy skeleton made them perfect for puffin hunting when that sort of thing was all the rage. Also they have six toes on each foot, which explains why they're such amazing piano players.

Norwich Terrier

Basically Norwich Terriers are
Norfolk Terriers but with pointy
ears. No, really. That's it.

Old English Sheepdog

A wonderfully bouncy and energetic breed. Love company and will follow you around all day. If you choose one as a companion, make sure you also buy a brush. You'll be needing it.

Otterhound

Huge and daft. They love water so much they prefer to drink from the bottom of a full bucket. Sadly, this impressive breed is now endangered.

Papillon

A petite, proud and pretty pet
that can pout as well as any
Parisian. Its name translates
as butterfly which is, of course,
a reference to its wonderful ears.
On a clear day you can see them
flying around the Eiffel Tower.

Patterdale Terrier

A bold yet soppy working dog.
The Patterdale likes to party, but
also to sit on your foot to keep
her posterior warm, and to
check you're not going anywhere
without her .

Peekapoo

These dainty little fellas have
been an established cross-breed
of Pekingese and Poodle for
around sixty years. They are
hypoallergenic, fluffy and
just love to bark. They look
and sound a bit like those
electronic dogs that do
backflips.

Pekingese

Chinese dog royalty. Legend tells us the Pekingese have strange origins. Apparently a lovesick lion was shrunk by divine powers so he could date and mate the marmoset of his dreams. Not your everyday love story then.

Peruvian Inca Orchid

This breed is more than a
thousand years old! Maybe
that's why it's sometimes
hairless and looks like a really
old man? So naked, it makes
other dogs blush.

Pharaoh Hound

Carvings from ancient Egyptian tombs reveal these dogs haven't changed in millennia. Yes, they always had those enormous pointy ears. They can read hieroglyphs fluently and work in schools teaching forgotten languages.

Plott

Brought to North Carolina in
1750 by the German Plott
brothers, one of whom died on
the trip over. Plotts are
lovable, clever and natural hunters.
In fact, if you don't fence them in,
they might just go hunting for a
raccoon, bear or coyote all by
themselves.

Pointer

Not just a pointer, but a tracker,
a hunter, a runner, a thinker,
possibly even a philosopher for all
we know. Pointing is really the
least of this dog's talents.

Pomeranian

These little puffballs were
once Arctic sled dogs but
that was when they were
bigger obviously. Bred to
be smaller companion dogs.
Famous owners apparently
include Queen Victoria,
Michelangelo and Sir
Isaac Newton!

Poodle

Poodles come in toy, miniature or standard styles. Actually very clever, active and useful dogs, as well as great entertainers, which must be why the French used them as performing circus dogs. Are often trimmed and coloured to resemble a pink topiary hedge.

Portuguese Water Dog

The fisherman's friend, able to
fish, retrieve broken nets and
doggy-paddle between boats
with messages. President
Obama's pet, Bo, is an
example of the breed, so
maybe this is how he sends
his top-secret communiqués?

Prairie Dog

Okay, so it's a dog by name,
not a dog by nature. In fact,
it's a kind of squirrel. But
it's furry, cute and likes to
dig holes, so why not?

Pug

Happy, affectionate and mischievous dogs. Pugs are masters of hypnotism; simply look into those big, dark, soulful eyes and you will be completely under their spell, at least until they start to wheeze, snort and snore.

Puli

An ancient breed from Hungary,
the Puli has been herding sheep
for over a thousand years which
may explain why it hasn't had
time to comb its hair. A
perennial puppy in attitude with
a dreadlock Rasta hairdo.

Redbone Coonhound

Where's them raccoons? This American red-coated breed is a hunter, a tracker and a swimmer. And with those ears, might just be a flyer, too.

Rhodesian Ridgeback

A loyal breed from South Africa.
Their name is thanks to a ridge
of hair on their spine that grows
in the opposite direction to the
rest of their coat. Originally bred
to help with hunting lions, so
they're either really brave or
really stupid.

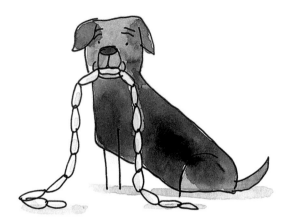

Rottweiler

An imposing and powerful
guard dog that dispersed
across Europe thanks to its
popularity with the Roman
army. Once favoured by
butchers in their home town
of Rottweil in Germany.
And, Indeed, they still are,
as the old saying goes, 'as
fit as a butcher's dog'.

Rough Collie

Like a Smooth Collie, but
er... rougher. An elegant,
affectionate Scottish breed,
with a beautiful long coat
that needs regular grooming.
Why such a thick coat? Have
you been to the Scottish
Highlands? Brrrr!

Saluki

One of the oldest breeds.
Known as the Royal Dog of
Egypt. They have rather
fabulous long and fluffy ears
and tails. Plus they have
extra-padded feet, making
for a very fancy looking
marathon runner.

Samoyed

Beloved by their nomadic masters, the Samoyeds and the Nentsy. A beautiful, snow-white Siberian breed with smiling, jet-black lips. They're adapted for the cold with wonderfully hairy toes. These gentle, intelligent dogs are the original Arctic explorers.

Schipperke

A Belgian chocolate of a dog.
Very elegantly presented, but too
many of them would be a bad idea.
They are known as the little
black fox as these fuzzballs can
be quite mischievous.

Schnauzer

Schnauzer literally means moustache. The female of the breed is a little embarrassed about this.

Schnoodle

What do you get if you cross a Schnauzer with a Poodle? A topiary hedge with a moustache.

Scottish Terrier

Elegant and compact. Trot along like dressage horses. Deeply suspicious of other dogs, all of which are considered lesser beings. If they were honest with themselves, can be quite grumpy.

Shar Pei

You know the one – with a
blue-black tongue – looking
like they're wearing a much
bigger dog's coat, all squidgy
and wrinkly. Their loose,
prickly coat helped protect
them in fights with other
animals in ancient China.
And the tongue? Well, that's
just a great party trick.

Shiba Inu

The smallest of Japan's native dogs, and a friend to other dogs, children and even cats. Likes to go mountain climbing on weekends.

Shih Tzu

Yes, yes, they've heard all the
jokes about their name.
Actually it translates as the
rather splendid Lion Dog. They
originate in Tibet where they
were developed by local monks
as head-warmers. Probably.

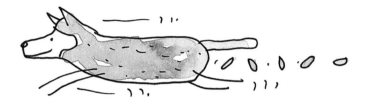

Siberian Husky

Strong, lively and energetic
dogs that are happy to sleep
outside in minus 104 degrees
fahrenheit. Will happily go to
the toilet while pulling a sled,
so be aware if you are driving.
Their crystal-coloured eyes
are actually lasers for cutting
through frozen ice.

Skye Terrier

Reputed to have Spanish and
Viking heritage they're one of
Scotland's oldest dogs, but are
a rare beast these days. Skyes
were a favourite of Queen
Victoria. Presumably Her
Royal Highness had to appoint
an extra court hairdresser?

Smooth Collie

Just like their fluffier
counterparts, this breed is clever,
loyal and will happily herd you
into a sheep pen. They have a
reputation as the fast ones
among collies. Smooth hair
makes you go faster apparently.

Spotted Hyena (wild dog)

This laughing scavenger is the
most common carnivore in
Africa. Living in clans of up
to a hundred individuals, with
females three times the size
of the males and therefore
firmly ruling the roost. And,
actually, they are more related
to cats than dogs. Who knew?!

Springer Spaniel

Utterly and fabulously crazy. Either deeply intelligent or completely stupid. Use crimping tongs to maintain eighties style hairdo.

St Bernard

A gentle giant that has become famous throughout history for Alpine rescues. The barrels are a bit of a myth, but who'd say no to a tot of brandy when stranded on a mountain ledge?

Staffordshire Bull Terrier

Loving and obedient, Staffies were originally used for blood sports like bull baiting because of their strength, stamina and courage. Is there anything physical they don't like? Well, they don't make great swimmers. But everything else is GAME ON!

Taco Terrier

A curious mix of Chihuahua
and Toy Fox Terrier which
results in big ears (really
big ears) and a quick mind.
Don't feed them Tacos,
by the way.

Talbot

Very popular dogs in
medieval Europe. This milk-
white hunting breed may be
an ancestor of the Beagle,
among others. They are all
gone now, though you can
still see them in England,
but only on pub signs.

Telomian

A breed from the Malaysian rainforest. Their original human companions used to live in houses on stilts because of all the snakes, scorpions and nasty insects. So Telomians developed an amazing climbing ability. Cats beware!

Tibetan Mastiff

This double - coated giant
is definitely royal: aloof,
solemn, a guardian of his
people and totally uninterested
in doing what he's told.

Tibetan Terrier

This sensitive breed has lived
with Buddhist monks for
centuries so must have
excellent karma.

Vizsla

This Hungarian breed is
great fun and has huge
amounts of boisterous energy
Vizslas can often be seen
galloping around the park at
full pelt before launching
themselves into a lake or
puddle. Were originally
companion dogs for
aristocracy, so they're
quite posh really.

Weimaraner

There's an ongoing debate about
whether they're dumb or just
have incredible focus. Rather like
an expensive car, they can be
buffed up with a chamois leather.

Welsh Corgi

Spirited yet loyal dogs. Unusually large ears, all the better for hearing with. The Queen's favourite and they know it.

West Highland White Terrier

The Westie has two natural states: cute and snappy. This plucky terrier isn't too keen on the whiteness of its hair and will roll in anything that promises to add some colour.

Whippet

Quiet, dignified, fast dogs
with excellent eyesight. Always
look a little chilly and a bit
worried. They love a race in
the park, especially with fat,
giddy Labradors.

Yellow Labrador

Okay, so Black, Brown and Yellow Labradors are not separate breeds, but are all just Labrador Retrievers of different colours. But we like them so much we thought they deserved separate entries. The yellow variety are super-chilled and also excellent at sniffing out illegal drugs. These facts are not related.

Yorkipoo

A cross between a Yorkshire
Terrier and a Poodle, of
course. But seriously, who
comes up with these names?
What about Yordle?
Or Porkshire? Or Pooshire?
Okay, maybe Yorkipoo isn't
so bad after all.

Yorkshire Terrier

Strong-minded, proud, often
vocal and quick to rise, that's
just the people of Yorkshire.
Their dogs are much the same.

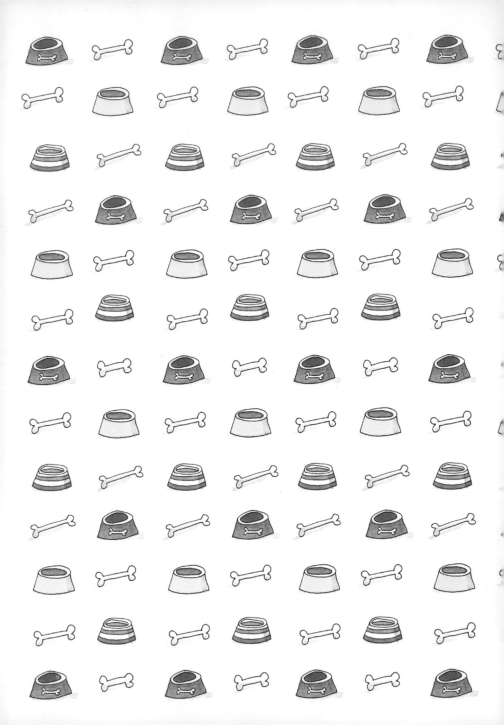